A LONELY GUY'S GUIDE

How to Deal

Hal Marcovitz

Copyright © 2015 by Enslow Publishers, Inc.

Library of Congress Cataloging-in-Publication Data

Marcovitz, Hal.
  [Guys' guide to loneliness]
  A lonely guy's guide : how to deal / Hal Marcovitz.
    pages cm. -- (A guy's guide)
  Originally published in 2008 as the author's A guys' guide to loneliness.
  Includes bibliographical references and index.
  Summary: "Explores the emotion of loneliness in young men and the best ways to deal with it and the situations that cause it. Includes real-life examples, quotes, facts, tips, and quizzes"--Provided by publisher.
    ISBN 978-1-62293-025-8—ISBN 978-1-62293-026-5 (pbk.)—ISBN 978-1-62293-027-2 (ePUB)—ISBN 978-1-62293-028-9 (PDF)—ISBN 978-1-62293-029-6 (PDF) 1. Loneliness. 2. Boys--Psychology. I. Title.
  BF575.L7M32 2014
  155.5'32—dc23
                                    2013015763

Future editions:
Paperback ISBN: 978-1-62293-026-5   EPUB ISBN: 978-1-62293-027-2
Single-User PDF ISBN: 978-1-62293-028-9   Multi-User PDF ISBN: 978-1-62293-029-6

Printed in the United States of America
072014 HF Group, North Manchester, IN
10 9 8 7 6 5 4 3 2 1

To Our Readers: We have done our best to make sure all Internet addresses in this book were active and appropriate when we went to press. However, the author and the publisher have no control over and assume no liability for the material available on those Internet sites or on other Web sites they may link to. Any comments or suggestions can be sent by e-mail to comments@enslow.com or to the address below.

Jasmine Health
Box 398, 40 Industrial Road
Berkeley Heights, NJ 07922
USA
www.jasminehealth.com

Illustration Credits: Shutterstock.com: Christos Georghiou (clipboard graphic), pp. 5, 20, 21, 30, 40, 46; Cory Thoman (brainstorm graphic), pp. 8, 52, 60; freesoulproduction (thumbtack graphic), pp. 6, 10, 15, 17, 27, 33, 34, 35, 37, 42, 54, 59; NLshop (therapist graphic), pp. 19, 31, 43, 45, 48, 53, 58, 61; Paris Owl, p. 1; Seamartini Graphics (atom graphic), pp. 11, 36, 37; vectorgirl (lightbulb graphic), pp. 16, 18, 51; zayats-and-zayats (quotation graphic), pp. 7, 22, 26, 32, 35, 51, 55.

Cover Photo: Paris Owl/Shutterstock.com

This book was originally published in 2009 as *A Guys' Guide to Loneliness*.

CONTENTS

CHAPTER ONE

Understanding Loneliness

> At his old school, Kyle had always been a good student. He had been on the school's track and soccer teams. And he had always had plenty of friends. But then his father found a new job and the family had to move to a new state.
>
> Kyle didn't know anyone at his new school, and no one seemed interested in him. He didn't try out for the soccer or track teams because he figured the coaches didn't know him and would cut him anyway. After school, he went straight home and up to his room. He felt lonely and miserable.

Everyone has felt lonely at one time or the other. Feelings of loneliness occur whenever you feel left out, forgotten, unneeded, and ignored. Feeling lonely is more than just being alone (which occurs when a person chooses to be by him- or herself). Loneliness is missing and longing for a connection with other people. Even though Kyle was in the middle of a crowd of kids at school, he felt very lonely because he really didn't know anyone.

The empty, lost feeling of being lonely can make anyone feel pretty bad. That's why it is often referred to as a negative emotion. Other negative emotions you can experience when lonely include anger, sadness, and grief. You're angry if you think other people aren't being friendly. You're sad because you think you have no friends. You feel grief over having lost old friendships.

Kyle's feelings of loneliness began after the move from his old neighborhood. The stress of being in a new situation affected his behavior. Because Kyle didn't know how to make friends at his new school, he avoided people. He walked to classes alone, and he ate by himself in the school cafeteria. Although he was a good athlete, he didn't try out for the school teams. He didn't want to make an embarrassing mistake in front of kids he didn't know. As he avoided talking

The Survey Says...

In a telephone survey of approximately a thousand high school students, the Horatio Alger Association found that 16 percent of respondents said a major problem for them was "feeling like no one understands" them. About 11 percent complained of "loneliness or feeling left out" as a major problem.

You and Your Emotions

A part of everyone's personality, emotions are a powerful driving force in life. They are hard to define and understand. But what is known is that emotions—which include anger, fear, love, joy, jealousy, and hate—are a normal part of the human system. They are responses to situations and events that trigger bodily changes, motivating you to take some kind of action.

Some studies show that the brain relies more on emotions than on intellect in learning and in making decisions. Being able to identify and understand the emotions in yourself and in others can help you in your relationships with family, friends, and others throughout your life.

with other kids, he felt ignored by them. He retreated into his own world and cut off contact with others.

Social loneliness. Kyle was suffering from social loneliness. That is, he no longer had a social group to hang out with. People who have a difficult time making friends typically suffer from social loneliness. And a big reason they have trouble making friends is shyness.

Shyness is that uncomfortable, self-conscious feeling you have when in a new situation or when meeting a stranger. Kyle had never thought of himself as shy before he moved. But he hadn't had much experience dealing with new situations or meeting new people. Now in a new place, he really didn't know what to say or do when he met strangers.

Emotional loneliness. Kyle was also suffering from emotional loneliness. He didn't feel close to anyone. There was no one he felt comfortable with to talk about what was on his mind. He was angry with his parents because of the move, so he didn't want to talk to them either.

With emotional loneliness you don't feel close to anyone—you have no one to share your thoughts and ideas with. You don't think anyone cares about you. And you don't think you can depend on anyone. You can also experience emotional loneliness even when you are part of a social group if you feel like you really can't be open or honest with anyone in that crowd.

"People are lonely because they build walls instead of bridges."
—Joseph Fort Newton

Quiz yourself

Loneliness can affect physical and mental health. Because of this, researchers at the University of California Los Angeles have developed the following Revised UCLA Loneliness Scale (RULS) to help health professionals determine whether their patients are lonely.

On a separate piece of paper, take the test. Indicate how often you have felt the way described in each statement using the following scale:

Scoring for questions in black:
4 = I have felt this way often.
3 = I have felt this way sometimes.
2 = I have rarely felt this way.
1 = I have never felt this way.

Scoring for questions in gray:
1 = I have felt this way often.
2 = I have felt this way sometimes.
3 = I have rarely felt this way.
4 = I have never felt this way.

1. I feel in tune with the people around me.

2. I lack companionship.

3. There is no one I can turn to.

4. I do not feel alone.

5. I feel part of a group of friends.

6. I have a lot in common with the people around me.

7. I am no longer close to anyone.

8. My interests and ideas are not shared by those around me.

9. I am an outgoing person.

10. There are people I feel close to.

11. I feel left out.

12. My social relationships are superficial.

13. No one really knows me well.

14. I feel isolated from others.

15. I can find companionship when I want it.

16. There are people who really understand me.

17. I am unhappy being so withdrawn.

18. People are around me but not with me.

19. There are people I can talk to.

20. There are people I can turn to.

*Health professionals consider a score of **20 points** to mean you don't feel lonely while **80 points** would indicate strong feelings of loneliness. Most people score around **40 points**. If your score is much higher than that, you should talk to a counselor or other trusted adult.*

Kyle was feeling both social and emotional loneliness because of his family's move. But many other things can affect whether a person feels lonely.

Causes of loneliness. Sometimes you can feel a bit lonely if you come home from school and there is no one around to talk to. You've finished your homework and chores, and you don't have any idea of what to do. Such bored, lonely feelings usually don't last long. They may be easily banished when you decide to call a friend, pick up a magazine or book, or go on the computer. You stop feeling lonely because you've become interested in something that has distracted you.

Lonely Feelings Often Occur When...

1. You have lost a relationship.
2. You feel unneeded and different from others.
3. You don't think you have friends.
4. You feel misunderstood.
5. You've recently moved.
6. You have poor relationships with family or peers.
7. You are extremely shy or lack social skills to make friends.

All humans need to connect with others. From birth onward, social interactions are essential for normal development—and for survival itself. Viennese psychiatrist René Spitz came to this conclusion during the 1940s after comparing children in an orphanage with those living in a prison nursery. The children living in the orphanage received little attention, although their surroundings were clean and they were well fed. However, these children not only displayed emotional and social disorders, but twenty-three of the eighty-eight institutionalized kids became sick and died. In contrast, all the children in the prison nursery—who were cuddled and able to form attachments with others—not only survived, but showed normal development.

Your personality can also affect whether or not you feel lonely. A situation that might make one person feel lonely could cause no problems at all for someone else. For example, if you have an outgoing personality, moving from your old neighborhood and changing schools might be easy for you. But if you are shy, you may have trouble trying to figure out unfamiliar social groups. Making new friends can be hard. One person may be devastated having lost the old familiar routine of life. Another person may react to change with excitement. Everyone is different.

Most people feel strong pangs of loneliness after the loss of something or someone important in their lives. You can feel pretty rotten after a conflict with a good friend or a breakup with a girlfriend. If a relationship has permanently ended, it can hurt—a lot. Another very hard kind of loss to deal with is the death of someone you care about. It is normal to feel intense loneliness after this kind of loss.

When people lose someone they care about, they may steer clear of future relationships. This way, they figure, they will not get hurt again. However, dealing with loneliness by withdrawing from people and not forming new friendships or relationships is not a good solution. Such actions are not healthy ways of coping with loss. Avoidance doesn't bring about solutions to problems. And it doesn't help you feel better.

Learning to cope. The teen years can be a tough time. At this time in your life, you are examining your values, trying new things, and reducing your emotional dependence on your parents. At the same time, you are establishing stronger and closer relationships with peers—the people of your own age. If those peers don't respond in a good way—if you feel rejected by them—it can be painful. After all, these are the people you are around the most and whose opinions you value.

At the same time, today's society makes it hard for boys to admit to having problems that cause emotional pain. Boys are expected to be "strong" and hide their emotions. This is especially true of emotions such as fear, hurt, or shame. These so-called negative emotions are thought to show weakness. However, it is important that you learn to understand and express your emotions, no matter what they are. Your emotions affect your behavior with others. When you understand and accept your feelings, you can work through your problems. Ultimately, you'll feel better about yourself and have healthier relationships with others.

It can be hard to come out of your shell when you are feeling lonely. But the first step in overcoming loneliness is recognizing that certain actions, such as withdrawing and avoiding, only make things worse. There are healthier ways to deal with feelings of loneliness and to overcome them.

CHAPTER TWO

The Shy Guy

> *During the first week of school, Isaiah noticed the new girl in his English class. In fact, everyone seemed to notice Kara, with her curly dark hair and ready smile.*
>
> *Since then, Kara has made a lot of friends in a short period of time. But Isaiah isn't one of them. Although he sits next to Kara in class, he hasn't really spoken to her. He thinks he'd like to get to know her. But whenever he looks her way, he freezes up and doesn't know what to say. He isn't sure how to break the ice.*

Isaiah isn't alone. Most people find that shyness gets in the way of making friends. It makes it hard to break the ice—to find the words to start a conversation with someone you don't really know. One out of two Americans admits that shyness is what keeps them from connecting with others.

What makes teens shy? The most common situations, teens say, are when they meet strangers, talk to authority figures, and try to talk to members of the opposite sex. Shyness causes a range of emotions.

The shy person feels uncomfortable, self-conscious, scared, or insecure. These feelings occur even before any conversation begins.

People who are mildly or moderately shy can usually work through their initial feelings of shyness in new situations. They force themselves to deal with their uncomfortable feelings. As they become involved in a conversation or speech, they generally find that their tense feelings disappear.

However, in the extremely shy person, such feelings don't melt away after a few minutes. It is too hard to push through the shyness. Extreme shyness can interfere with a person's ability to make friends or to

Shyness

Shyness often worsens during times of change. For example, you may feel really shy on the first day of school. Or you are more likely to have shy feelings when meeting someone new. This can be especially true when you're attracted to the person. You also are more likely to feel shy in new situations in which you don't understand what is expected of you.

To "break the ice" means to remove the awkwardness or tension of a first meeting. The expression, which dates back more than 400 years, refers to the breaking up of river ice during the spring thaw. After warm temperatures melted the ice, boats on the river could pass through to their destinations.

date. Such feelings can prevent people from becoming who they want to be.

When shyness is a problem. For many teens, extreme shyness can make them feel very isolated and alone. Because they don't think they can hold a conversation, they stop trying to talk. They become so overwhelmed with worry about what others might think of them that they don't speak up. They don't try new things, for fear of drawing attention to themselves.

The discomfort caused by shyness is easy to see in some people. They stammer and stutter as they try to find the right words. Their mistakes make them more nervous. They blush a lot or sweat heavily. In a new social situation, they may feel so embarrassed that all they can think about is how to escape the conversation or situation. Because talking to strangers is so painful, many extremely shy people simply retreat into their shells. They avoid social situations.

What Causes Shyness

Genes. Genes are units of heredity that help determine people's characteristics. Some scientists say the genes that children inherit from their parents can determine whether or not the kids are naturally shy. The shy personality can be apparent even when a person is very young. For example, shyness can keep a toddler from joining in a group activity right away. He or she may need to watch what's going on for a while before feeling comfortable joining in.

Learned behaviors. The way a person has been taught to handle social situations can affect whether he or she feels shy. If the parents are uncomfortable in social situations, the child may also be uneasy. If the parents have difficulty talking to new people, the child may imitate the same behavior without even realizing it.

Previous experiences. If a person has been treated badly in the past, he or she will be shy around others. Someone who has been teased, bullied, or humiliated will tend to avoid situations in which such things could happen again.

One out of ten people can experience extreme shyness, anxiety, and stress called social phobia. Feelings of fear are so strong that they interfere with the person's ability to relate to others. When untreated, the person with social phobia withdraws and avoids other people, so the disorder tends to grow worse. Treatment typically involves therapy. The person learns new social skills and ways to manage anxiety and reduce stress.

Some shy teens may appear calm and self-confident on the outside. But they are actually terribly nervous and unhappy on the inside. That's because they can't stop thinking about how they look. Or they are worrying about how the conversation is going. Or they are wondering whether the person they are talking to likes them. The fear of being embarrassed in social situations can make shy people come across as abrupt and unfriendly. (Although fortunately, it is possible to learn how to respond differently in such situations.)

Certain situations cause a physical response in the person who feels extreme shyness. This response is the fear reaction. In a social situation, the body and mind are reacting to an apparent danger. The danger is not real. But the fear reaction can cause a racing heart rate, weak knees, dizziness, and clammy hands. Symptoms of shyness can also include having a queasy feeling in the abdomen. This pain is often referred to as having "butterflies in the stomach."

Low self-esteem. Many shy people suffer from low self-esteem. The term self-esteem refers to the way you feel and think about yourself. If you have

Using "People Skills"

Be prepared. Practice what you are going to say before beginning a conversation. That way, the words will come more easily to you when you want to start talking.

Be aware of your body language. Be approachable. Remember that body language can make a shy person seem angry or rude. Try to act friendly, even when you are feeling very nervous—or left out. Face the speaker and look into his or her eyes. Be relaxed, but pay close attention.

When talking to a person, maintain eye contact. Show you are interested in what the person has to say. As the person speaks, try to feel what he or she is feeling. Keep an open mind.

Make it clear you are listening. Don't interrupt. Nod your head as the person speaks and say, "uh huh." If you don't understand something, wait until the speaker pauses and then ask him or her to explain. ("What do you mean by...?")

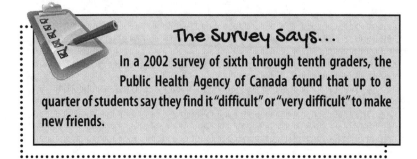
low self-esteem, you don't believe you have much to offer others. You may think that people don't want you around.

A guy with low self-esteem may think there is something wrong with him. He thinks that explains why people don't like him. Because he doesn't like himself, he figures no one is going to like him, either. Even when people act friendly toward him, he may suspect their motives. The shy guy may think that the only reason they're paying any attention to him is because they want something. He may think that they don't really like him for who he is.

Overcoming shyness. You may believe that you fall into the category of the extremely shy person. However, you can still make friends. The first step is to recognize your shy feelings and then push through them. One way to do that is to work on improving your "people skills." These are the techniques you can use when interacting with others.

Work at making small talk. If you don't feel competent making conversation, listen in on the small talk others are having. Then, once you think you have the right idea, force yourself to practice these same skills.

When you have a conversation, try not to be self-conscious. But make sure your body language shows you are interested in what the other person is saying: look him or her in the eye. When you look at the floor, you are sending a signal that says you don't care what the other person is saying. Stand up straight and tall

Some Strategies Used by Teens to Overcome Shyness

- "Tried making conversation with people I would like to know." (72 percent)
- "Tried going to public places (e.g., mall, dances, park) to meet people." (44 percent)
- "Joined activities outside school." (39 percent)
- "Joined clubs or extracurricular activities in school." (37 percent)
- "Used alcohol or drugs." (24 percent)
- "Had individual therapy or counseling." (8 percent)
- "Read self-help books." (4 percent)

Percentages do not add up to 100 percent because the survey allowed for the selection of more than one strategy. From Bernardo J. Carducci et al., "How Shy Teens Deal With Shyness: Strategic and Gender Differences," Poster Session, American Psychological Association, Toronto, Canada, August 2003.

and smile. Even if you don't feel confident, do your best to look like you are feeling self-assured and in control. Try to act like you are comfortable with the situation (even if you're not). You may find that with time—and practice—you actually will become a little more relaxed in new social situations.

You can find opportunities to practice by joining an after-school club or activity that involves groups of people. But don't join just any club. Pick one that involves something you like to do. For example, if you like playing chess, join the chess club at school. Conversations should go easier when you share common interests.

Be prepared. When you know a possibly uncomfortable social situation is coming up, practice ahead of time. Plan what you'll say or do. For example,

"The worst loneliness is not to be comfortable with yourself."
—Mark Twain

if you are thinking of asking the girl in your science class if she'd like to go to the school dance with you, rehearse what you'll say next time you see her. You could write down what you want to say. Or you could practice the conversation in front of the mirror. Be sure to take the next step, though, and actually follow through on that conversation.

Think positive. Try to stop being so hard on yourself. Don't think negative thoughts about how you look or imagine the bad things that others may be thinking about you. Find something positive about yourself. What are you good at? What are your qualities and strengths? Be your own best friend. You would want to give a good friend some support before he or she tried a difficult task, right? Treat yourself the same way. When you are about to deal with a potentially uncomfortable situation, give yourself a compliment and encouragement.

Be assertive. Being assertive means standing up for and expressing what you believe in. But it also means being respectful of others' opinions and beliefs. Being assertive can be hard for the shy person who is caught up with worry about what other people are thinking. But if you believe strongly in something, you need to speak up in an assertive way. You will feel better about yourself.

Avoid avoidance. Sure, it may be easier to avoid situations that make you uncomfortable. But doing that won't help you learn how to cope with shy feelings. By putting yourself forward into situations that make you feel shy—and forcing yourself to stay in them—you will get used to them. Replace old patterns of avoiding conversations with new experiences of participating in them. With practice, you may find it easier to think of things to say. These behaviors you learn and practice today will help you for the rest of your life.

CHAPTER THREE

Building Friendships

Afriend is someone you can relax with and be yourself. Friends can be a source of fun—people to share good times with. And friends can provide understanding, support, and guidance when you're having trouble. During the teen years, you can often be more comfortable talking with friends rather than with family about issues and problems. You may find you relate better with friends because friends often are going through the same kinds of situations and having similar feelings.

However, if you have difficulty making and keeping friends, some of the suggestions in this chapter can help. Keep them in mind the next time you are talking to classmates and other peers. Remember, what is most important in forming relationships with other

> "A real friend is one who walks in when the rest of the world walks out."
> —Walter Winchell

people is that you be yourself. Don't pretend to be someone you're not.

Initiate the conversation. If you see someone you'd like to get to know better, make the first move. Say hello and smile. Make a comment about the upcoming class test, yesterday's basketball game, or even the weather. Don't wait for the other person to talk first.

Show you are interested in what the other person is saying. Once a conversation has begun, continue it by asking questions and listening to the answers. Ask the other person about what he or she thinks. People appreciate it when you show an interest in them and what they have to say. Learn to be a good listener.

Give and take. Share your own thoughts and opinions. But be respectful when others have ideas and opinions that differ from yours. You don't want to make friends only with people who think exactly like you do, although it is likely you'll be attracted to people who share your values.

Choose your friends wisely. Every school has its groups or cliques. They typically form when teens with similar interests, values, and personalities hang out together. They may join a group because they feel comfortable with its members. But sometimes teens look to join groups for the wrong reasons—to be with the guys who are thought to be popular or who are top athletes.

Characteristics of a Good Friend

- Can be trusted not to betray a confidence
- Shows an interest in you and is concerned about your problems
- Is supportive and helps out when needed
- Celebrates your successes
- Is honest
- Has a good sense of humor

Take your time in choosing your friends. Avoid joining a group simply because it has an identity you think you'd like to have. And don't keep company with people you don't really like or respect—just because you think no one else is around.

Instead, try to develop friendships with people who are supportive and understanding. Avoid people who constantly tease you or make you feel bad about yourself. Don't make friends with people who like to gossip about others or put them down. You may find that you become the object of their harassment. Similarly, steer clear of those who try to make you do things that you don't want to do or that you think are wrong.

Building good friendships takes time. Remember, being good friends with a person involves sharing a part of yourself. It involves both giving and receiving trust. That means you don't talk about your friend with others. And you don't expect that friend to talk about you, either. If a friend has told you something in confidence, you don't tell other people unless you are concerned for the friend's safety. In that case, you should tell a parent or other trusted adult.

CHAPTER FOUR

Feeling Rejected and Depressed

> Seth has been unhappy since the first day of middle school, when for some reason he got on the bad side of Kevin and his friends. At school, they picked on Seth for being so bad at sports. But the teasing was worse when he was at home on the computer. At Kevin's prompting, other kids from school bombarded Seth's computer with insulting messages. Someone posted an embarrassing picture of him on a Web site.

Being rejected by peers hurts. And the sadness and isolation that a victim of bullying feels can hurt a lot. The effects of feeling isolated and rejected can last a long time—well into adulthood.

Being bullied. Bullying can be physical assaults such as hitting, punching, or shoving. Or it can involve having one's belongings taken or damaged. It can also be verbal assaults such as name-calling, teasing, or threats of physical abuse. A more recent form of bullying is cyberbullying. It involves teasing, insults, and threats that are text-messaged on cell phones or that appear on Web sites.

Bullies often pick on kids who are seen as different. The victim of bullying may be overweight or have a disability. A guy may be picked on because he's not athletic or because he's seen as being "too smart." Regardless of the "reason" for being bullied, the victim feels deep pain and loneliness because of rejection. Often the guy who is the victim of bullying blames himself. He thinks that there must be something wrong with him. It is hard for him to realize the truth—that the problem is with the bully, not with him.

When bullying goes on for a long time, it makes its victim feel isolated and alone. Kids who are subjected to months and years of bullying figure they have no alternative but to avoid situations where it takes place. So they often skip school or simply drop out.

The Survey Says...

According to the U.S. Department of Health and Human Services, approximately 15 to 25 percent of U.S. students say they are bullied frequently. Another 15 to 20 percent say that they bully others.

If You Are Being Bullied

1. Don't keep your feelings to yourself. Talk to a trusted friend or adult.

2. Be aware that the bullying is not likely to go away on its own.

3. Confront the bully and ask her or him to stop, if you feel safe doing that.

4. If the bullying continues, talk to an adult about what is going on.

Depression and loneliness. Being tormented and teased by bullies can wear anyone down. If you're constantly hearing negative comments about yourself, you can easily begin to believe what is being said and lose confidence in yourself. Ongoing feelings of loneliness and low self-esteem can lead to even more serious problems such as major depression.

Clinical depression is a form of major depression. It is diagnosed when feelings of extreme sadness last for more than two weeks. A guy with clinical depression is typically in a sad mood all the time. He is irritable and has feelings of hopelessness.

"It is loneliness that makes the loudest noise. This is true of men as of dogs."
—Eric Hoffer

Other symptoms of clinical depression may include emotional instability, extreme mood swings, and the lack of ability to focus on daily tasks. Some psychologists believe that symptoms of depression for men can also include angry outbursts, withdrawal, and risk-taking behaviors.

Because men and boys are socialized to not show emotions, they try to ignore them. If they are suffering from severe depression, trying to ignore emotions can be a serious problem. Psychologist William Pollack notes, "Men not only don't get treatment, they try to convince themselves they don't have an illness." Because they don't acknowledge their pain, guys tend to express negative feelings with violence. They may direct it toward themselves with self-destructive behavior and recklessness. Or they may act violently toward others. In some cases, they turn to drugs to "self-medicate" their emotional pain.

In teenagers, depression often occurs with other disorders such as anxiety, eating disorders, and substance abuse. Depression has also been found to lead to increased risk for suicide. Men commit suicide at four times the rate than that of women, a statistic that to some experts means symptoms of depression in men and boys aren't being recognized.

Cynically Shy

Researcher Bernardo Carducci reports that the connection between shyness and bullying doesn't apply only to shy teens being targets. He found that certain teens are what the researchers call "cynically shy." That is, their shyness not only makes them uncomfortable, but angry. As a result, they turn into bullies themselves. "They feel frustrated and hostile because they can't connect," Carducci says. "When you feel that isolated, you can begin to have hostile feelings toward others. . . . And it's very easy to go from hating people to hurting people." The researcher believes that some cynically shy teens have gone on to horrific acts, including shootings in schools.

Clinical Depression

Bullying is not the only stressful situation that can lead to depression. People typically feel sad when other difficult crises occur, such as a parent's divorce, breakup with a good friend, or the death of a loved one. In most cases, the result will be a bad mood and a short period of feeling down. However, when depression lasts for more than two weeks, it is considered clinical depression.

Major depression is treatable. Studies have shown that the most effective treatment is a combination of medications and psychotherapy, or "talk therapy." Through one form of talk therapy, a medical professional works with the patient to try to change negative styles of thinking and behaving. Another kind of therapy involves helping the patient improve troubled personal relationships.

If you think you may have problems with depression or you have a friend whom you believe is suffering from depression, you should talk to an adult. He or she can help you or your friend obtain help from a trained mental health professional. This person can figure out what is causing the depression and prescribe appropriate therapy or medication.

Signs of Depression

These symptoms usually occur every day over a period of at least two weeks:

Emotional: prolonged sadness, emptiness, low self-esteem, guilt, or thoughts of suicide and death.

Physical: sleep and appetite disorders, headaches, or stomachaches.

Behavioral: isolating self from others; acting out anger; conflicts with friends, parents, or at school; turning to alcohol or drug abuse.

"Young & the Lonely: A Team of Top Experts Answers Your Questions About Loneliness and Depression," *Science World,* February 7, 2003

"Always keep an open mind and a compassionate heart."

—Phil Jackson

Take action against feelings of loneliness. Many guys detach themselves from a situation when they face problems. They find it difficult to discuss their feelings with others, considering it a sign of weakness. But they need to recognize that admitting to their feelings is actually a courageous thing to do.

Even though it may be difficult, try to talk to others about what you are experiencing. Push yourself to talk to somebody else about the way you feel. Don't shut yourself off from family and friends, but instead try to reach out and improve your relationship with at least

⚛⚛⚛ **Science Says...** ⚛⚛⚛

Depression is a biochemical disorder that affects the body's neurotransmitters. Neurotransmitters are special chemicals that carry messages between brain cells in the brain. Depression occurs when neurotransmitters such as serotonin and dopamine, which affect the emotions, are out of balance. The disorder requires quick medical attention.

⚛ ⚛ ⚛ Science Says... ⚛ ⚛ ⚛

Loneliness can be bad for your health. Psychology professor John Cacioppo and researchers from the University of Chicago and Ohio State University have reported that lonely people have a harder time handling stress than people who aren't lonely. They tend to feel threatened, rather than challenged, by stressful situations. The feeling of being threatened leads to high blood pressure, which in turn affects heart function and disrupts sleep.

Unhealthy Ways of Coping

There are several unhealthy ways of dealing with loneliness. Some guys deny there is a problem at all. They don't try to form relationships or make friends. Instead, they may obsess over celebrities and sports stars or spend all their free time in front of the television set or computer. Some people may try to escape from unhappy or lonely feelings by using drugs or alcohol.

one other person, especially a person whom you trust. Ask for feedback from others about whether your behavior could be contributing to your problems with others. Ask for advice on what to do.

Be open and willing to accept that person's thoughts. And follow through. If you don't try to take some kind of positive action, it is possible things can become worse. Instead of allowing loneliness to lead to anger or hostility, you can ease your feelings when you talk about them. When you connect with your problem, you have a better likelihood of finding a solution

CHAPTER FIVE

When Loss Causes Loneliness

Jason is having a hard time. Last year, his father moved out of the house, and a few months ago, his parents' divorce was finalized. Although Jason sees his father on weekends, he misses spending time with him. Meanwhile, his mother has much less time to spend with either Jason or his little brother. She is often too busy with her new job and with chores to talk to Jason. He misses the times when the whole family used to sit down together at the dinner table, and often wishes his life would return to the way it used to be.

When you lose someone who is important to you, it can leave a hole in your life. Jason feels sad and lonely because the divorce means he no longer sees his father every day. Feelings of loneliness can occur because of other kinds of life changes, too, such as the death of a close family member or friend or a breakup with someone important to you. Such events can cause a range of emotions, including sadness and fear—as well as emotional loneliness.

Loss because of divorce. It is estimated that each year the parents of one million American kids get divorced. In total, some 20 million kids under the age of eighteen live in homes in which their parents have decided to separate or divorce. In other words, there are a lot of kids like Jason.

If you are dealing with your parents' separation or divorce, you may also be experiencing loneliness and depression. You may feel that your parents are too wrapped up in their problems. Or that they aren't there to connect with you and your needs. Even if the divorce has been over and done with for many years, you still may feel isolated from your parents.

Sometimes kids whose parents are divorcing blame themselves for the breakup. Because they believe the divorce is their fault, they avoid talking about it and how it makes them feel. As a result, they can feel terribly lonely and isolated. It is important to

The Survey Says...

According to statistics for 2002, 10 percent of the American population is divorced, up from 8 percent in 1990 and 6 percent in 1980.

remember that when separations and divorces occur, they happen because of the couple's problems with each other. Breakups are not the fault of the kids.

Dealing with changes. Many changes in family life can occur because of divorce. Depending on the custody agreement, visits with one parent may be limited. As a result, you won't see as much of one of your parents as you did before the divorce. You may be shuttling back and forth between both your mother's place and your father's home. Or you may be living with only one parent. One or both of your parents may have remarried. That means you may be having to learn to deal with a whole new set of family members—stepsiblings or half-brothers and half-sisters.

In addition, the separation and divorce may have caused financial problems for the parent you live with. Without the income of both parents, there may not be enough money to support the household. This may mean you and your family have to move to where housing is less expensive.

A new family situation and moving to a new neighborhood are major changes. When you must deal with a lot of changes, you can feel a great deal of stress. And if at the same time you don't think anyone cares about what you are going through, it can be really hard. That's where feelings of loneliness can kick in—when you feel like you have no one to talk to. No one understands what you are going through.

Psychologists believe that divorce can be very difficult on boys, who often live with the mothers as the result of custody decisions. The divorce can mean a son spends little time with his father. Instead of expressing feelings of disappointment over no longer living with their dad, many boys feel as though they have to "tough it out." They don't talk about how they feel isolated and lonely. Additional pressure to "side with" their mother or become the man of the house can also contribute to feelings of aloneness, alienation from Dad, and being different from other guys.

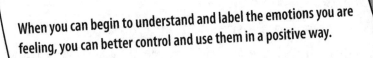

When you can begin to understand and label the emotions you are feeling, you can better control and use them in a positive way.

Helping Others Cope With Loss

If you have a friend who has recently broken up with someone, you can provide support to make the person feel better. Offer your support and companionship. But let your friend do most of the talking. Be aware that he or she will be moody—filled with grief, anger, confusion, and negative feelings. Let your friend know that you understand and will be there if needed.

Although it can be uncomfortable being around someone going through pain and difficulty, your presence can mean a lot. It shows your friend that he or she is not alone.

Grief and loss. Feelings of isolation and loneliness can be particularly strong after the death of a family member or close friend. When someone close to you dies, you lose having the person around and involved in your life. Your reaction can vary. The initial shock can overwhelm you with terrible grief, or the sense of missing the person may come in waves that occur at unexpected times. Or you may be surprised to find you react with very little emotion. Such feelings are all normal, although painful.

Grief is a normal and healthy reaction to loss. It is normal to cry and feel sad and depressed when someone close to you dies. Grieving the death of a loved one doesn't mean you are suffering from major depression. However, coping with your sorrow can take time—weeks, months, and even years.

Psychologist Elisabeth Kübler-Ross observed the feelings of people with terminal illnesses or experiencing the death of loved ones. She described these feelings of grief as occurring in five stages:

Denial: "This can't be happening."

Anger: "Why is this happening? Whose fault is it?"

Bargaining: "I promise to _____, if my friend lives."

Depression: "I'm too sad to do anything."

Acceptance: "What has happened or will happen can't be changed. I'm at peace with it and ready to move on."

It is necessary to go through the stages of grief—as painful as they can be—according to your own schedule in order to come to terms with your loss.

Loss with the breakup of a relationship. The same feelings of grief and loneliness that occur with the death of someone close to you can also occur with the breakup of a relationship. It is normal to feel lonely

When to Get Help

It's time to get help if a friend experiences any of the following:

- Spends an excessive amount of time alone
- Shows a lack of interest in daily activities
- Experiences changes in sleeping and eating habits
- Uses drugs or alcohol to numb feelings
- Threatens to harm himself or herself
- Engages in risky behavior

when a relationship—whether a close friendship or a romantic relationship—comes to an end.

When someone you love and care about has chosen to break up with you, your sense of loss can be overwhelming. Feelings of numbness and disbelief that the breakup has occurred are followed by pain. You may feel physically sick, lose your appetite, and have difficulty concentrating on other things. Eventually, feelings of anger against the person give way to loneliness and despair. It's natural to start longing for the way things used to be.

It can be hard to think well of yourself if the other person is the one deciding it was time to break up. This can be especially true when you weren't even aware of a problem. As a result, some guys turn on themselves when a relationship ends. They believe that if they had only been smarter, better looking, or richer, then things would have worked out.

Keep in mind that breakups seldom occur because of one reason or character trait. More typically they occur because at least one of you has changed. Rather than spend energy obsessing over how to renew a lost relationship, acknowledge it is over and move on. Be patient with yourself. With time, you'll be able to think better about tomorrow. Getting over a breakup can take a matter of days or it can take months—the amount of time you need depends on how you deal with your emotions and on how strong or important the relationship was to you.

Coping with loss. Your emotional reactions to loss are normal, but you may be feeling overwhelmed by them. To stay healthy during such stressful times, it is important that you take care of yourself.

To minimize the effects of stress on your body, take care of yourself physically. Get lots of sleep, eat healthy foods, and exercise regularly. You'll still be sad, but staying healthy can help you avoid becoming severely depressed. Keep yourself busy—work on a hobby, get together with friends to watch a movie or play a basketball game, listen to music, or go for a run.

You will need to think about what happened, but try not to dwell on your loss. Deal directly with your feelings and try to "process" them. Pay attention to your emotions. Name what you are feeling and accept that it exists. Then, after holding and accepting the feeling for a few minutes, consciously try to let it go.

For example, you may identify that you are feeling angry. Consciously acknowledging the anger will help you see how it is affecting your behavior. Perhaps you are pushing people away because you are lashing out at them. So they are steering clear of you. As a result of your behavior, your feelings of isolation and loneliness are intensifying. Once you process that you are feeling angry, you can try to change your behavior—and reconnect with others who may be able to help you.

What you don't want to do is to try to deaden the pain of loss by using alcohol or drugs. To get over the pain of loss, you need to deal with it. When you use alcohol and drugs instead of working through your emotions, you are numbing yourself to your feelings. They will continue to build up inside and stay with you. Using alcohol and drugs don't provide long-lasting solutions. They only invite more problems since their use by teens is also illegal.

To help lessen the pain of loneliness caused by loss, talk to other people. By sharing your feelings with someone who understands what you're going through, you'll feel better. This person can be a good friend or family member you can easily talk to. Your

Sharing feelings can be tough for guys. You may feel more comfortable talking to a female friend or relative, such as an older sister. Or you may find it helpful to talk to a school counselor, psychologist, or a clergy person. Sometimes, just hanging out with friends can help take your mind off the hurt and any negative feelings you are having.

problems need to be heard, and when you share your concerns with others, you may also hear advice that you hadn't thought of.

As with the pain caused by breakups, the grief caused by loss will be helped with the passage of time. You can also benefit by accepting and working through the emotions you are feeling.

CHAPTER SIX

Choosing to Be Alone

> When Jake is done with school each day, he comes home to an empty house. His mother, who now works the evening shift, had asked him if he would have preferred going to a friend's house after school each day instead. But at age thirteen, Jake feels okay with the way things are. Every day, as soon as he walks through the door, he makes sure to call his mother to let her know he's home. Then he typically grabs a bite to eat, takes the dog for a walk, and takes care of chores. He figures that if he doesn't take care of his responsibilities, his parents might not want him home after school by himself anymore. And he likes having time alone.

Just because you are alone doesn't mean you are lonely. Many kids with working parents spend time by themselves when they come home from school. This time by themselves can be a real plus. It can give them a chance to think without interruption, read, study, or work on homework or hobbies.

There are other ways you might choose solitude— time when you are alone. Sometimes you might prefer

> Solitude is the state of being alone and secluded from other people. It typically occurs because of a conscious choice to be alone.

to stay at home rather than attend the school dance or attend a movie with the rest of your friends. You might prefer to spend the time doing something on your own—reading a book, playing music, or writing a computer program.

Just wanting to be by yourself doesn't make you lonely. Feelings of loneliness occur when you are sad about the situation. Someone who chooses to be alone doesn't feel unhappy and wish things were different.

> "I never found the companion that was so companionable as solitude."
> —Henry David Thoreau

Are You an Extrovert or Introvert?

An Extrovert:

... is talkative and open.

... likes to think out loud.

... shows emotions.

... acts before thinking.

... likes to be with people.

... has lots of energy.

... is outgoing.

An Introvert:

... is quiet and thoughtful.

... listens more than talks.

... keeps emotions private.

... thinks before acting.

... prefers to work "behind-the-scenes."

... likes to spend time alone.

... is reserved.

Extroverts and introverts. Personality plays a part in how you feel about being by yourself. There are two main kinds of personalities: the extrovert and the introvert. Extroverts are outgoing individuals who thrive in crowded situations and enjoy working in busy, stimulating environments. They gain energy by being among people. However, they tend to feel very lonely and drained when they have to spend a lot of time alone.

When You're Home Alone

If you are home alone after school and find yourself a little bored and lonely, you can always find something to do. Things to do can include

- Homework
- Chores
- Reading a book or magazine
- Working on a hobby
- Listening to or playing music
- Writing a letter
- Phoning a friend
- Using the computer

Too Much Time Alone on the Computer?

Some people are concerned that teens are spending too much time on online activities such as multi-user games, instant messaging, and chat rooms. Some studies show that introverted kids who excessively play online games based on role-playing (acting out the role of another character) become isolated from friends and peers.

According to a study by the Stanford Institute for the Quantitative Study of Society, the more time people spend online, the less time they give to real-life relationships with family and friends. One of the study's authors blamed the Internet for having "an increasingly isolating effect on society."

Others disagree. They point out that while 36 percent of Americans log on to the computer for more than five hours per week, approximately 60 percent of them say they spend less time watching TV. In addition, using e-mail was the most popular activity. In other words, the Internet defenders say, people are more connected with friends and family because of e-mail.

In contrast, introverts like spending time alone, although they are not necessarily shy or lonely. They get energy from being on their own rather than being with large groups of people. When in crowds, they often feel drained of energy. Introverts like to work alone, rather than in groups. Solitude allows them to pursue activities such as writing, drawing, or painting.

Time for independent thinking. Working alone can help you become an independent thinker. There is nothing wrong with working with others—that builds an appreciation for teamwork. However, a lot can be said for learning how to do things on your own. By working alone, you have a chance to develop and nurture your own ideas.

Solitude can be a time when you review your thoughts and goals and decide what is important to

"Man's loneliness is but his fear of life."
—Eugene O'Neill

you. When you work on a project on your own, you can also gain confidence in yourself and your abilities to finish something on your own. Being on your own can also give you the opportunity to show that you can take care of yourself.

Time for creativity. In a 2005 survey, Americans were asked to finish the sentence, "My most creative ideas come when…" More than half of the respondents chose "in solitude" as the answer. Most experts agree that solitude provides the quiet time that gives people the opportunity to come up with creative solutions to problems. That "alone time" provides a time for insights and for following wherever your own natural curiosity and imagination take you. Studies find that creative, imaginative people such as artists, musicians, and writers are at their most productive when they work alone.

Taking time out. Many psychologists believe that people benefit when they have the chance to take "time out" and be on their own. This time spent away from other people can give them the opportunity to take an "emotional breather." They can think about themselves and their relationships with others. Or they can practice a favorite hobby. In general, having time to yourself can give you the opportunity to think without distractions from others.

CHAPTER SEVEN

Overcoming Loneliness

Loneliness can affect you in many different ways. You can feel a little lonely when you're simply bored and not sure what you want to do with yourself. And you can feel extremely lonely if you feel rejected and unwanted. A lack of friends may make you think something is wrong with you, which in turn can make you self-conscious, ill at ease, or even angry with others. A breakup or the death of a close friend or family member can result in feelings of loneliness, as well as anger, sadness, and grief.

So what do you do? If your loneliness is the result of wanting a close friendship or relationship, many of the same tips for overcoming shyness apply: these tips

Tips for Overcoming Loneliness

- Be aware of how you relate to others.
- Practice your people skills.
- Be the one to start a conversation.
- Get involved in classroom discussions and conversations.
- Don't avoid social situations. In fact, go out of your way to meet new people.

for overcoming loneliness boil down to developing the social skills that help you form close relationships.

Remember, the more people you talk to, the better the odds of finding a good friend. Schools have many clubs, sports teams, and other extracurricular activities. Look for an activity that interests you and join. Not only will you meet new people, but you'll find friends who share the same interests.

You can also meet new people and practice interpersonal skills by working in a service job. In the restaurant business, for example, you have contact with many different people in a somewhat structured environment. You may also have the opportunity

Ways That Teens Cope with Loneliness

Teens say that they use various ways to cope with loneliness—some are helpful and some are harmful. The unhealthy ways do nothing to help solve the problem.

Harmful
- *Feel sad and withdraw:* Cry, sleep, watch TV, do nothing.
- *Try to numb bad feelings:* Turn to drugs or alcohol.
- *Spend money:* Buy things to make themselves feel better.

Helpful
- *Seek solitude:* Work, read, write, listen to music, exercise, get involved with a hobby.
- *Give self pep talks:* Say things like, "These feelings won't last forever," and "I have good qualities that someone will see."
- *Reach out to others:* Call or visit a friend, help someone, or join a new activity.

to learn skills on how to deal with people who are different from you.

One of the best ways to overcome your own loneliness, experts say, is by helping others. By spending time with other people, especially those living in assisted care or hospitals, you can help reduce their feelings of loneliness. Be a volunteer in a service organization and do something to help out in your community. As you increase your contact with other people, you won't feel as isolated. And at the same

Is Your Behavior Ruining Friendships?

1. Do you get angry with others easily?

2. When you are with a group of friends and they decide to play ball when you would rather do something else, do you go home instead of joining in the game?

3. Instead of letting minor problems pass, do you hold a grudge?

4. When you are angry with your friends, do you give them the silent treatment?

5. Be honest. Would you like to be friends with the person who answers "yes" to all of these questions?

Conversation Starters

Ask open-ended questions (questions that require more than yes or no for an answer). Instead of saying, "Do you like that television show?" (easily answered by yes or no), say "Why do you think that show is such a big hit?"

time, you will feel good about yourself for helping to make the world a better place.

Keep your existing friendships healthy. Be aware of your behavior—are you acting like the kind of friend you would want to have? If not, clean up your act. Do your best to be there for your friends when they need you.

Go out of your way to talk to friends and family members. Although you may enjoy hobbies such as watching television, reading books, and surfing the Internet, be sure to take time to live in the real world. Participate in your school and community activities and visit people you care about.

Remember that everyone has feelings of loneliness at one time or another. Even those people who seem very confident and self-assured will admit to feeling lonely and scared about certain things. If you're nervous about starting a conversation with the student standing next to you in the lunch line, keep in mind that the other person is probably feeling as self-conscious or uncertain as you are.

If you've spent your life avoiding situations that make you uncomfortable, forcing yourself to behave differently can feel like taking a step off a cliff. But if you believe you aren't any good at making friends, then you probably won't be! Practice replacing those negative thoughts with more positive ones. And keep trying to connect and get to know new people. With persistence, you are bound to find the people with whom you feel really comfortable. So, stay active and keep reaching out to others.

Books

Brantley, Jeffrey, and Wendy Millstine. *Mindful Practices to Help You Overcome Loneliness, Connect With Others, and Cultivate Happiness.* Oakland, Calif.: New Harbinger Publications, 2011.

Greenberger, Robert. *Frequently Asked Questions About Loneliness.* New York: Rosen Pub Group, 2007.

Internet Addresses

TeensHealth: Mind

http://teenshealth.org/teen/your_mind/

National Institute of Mental Health: Depression

http://www.nimh.nih.gov/health/topics/depression/index.shtml

Hotlines

National Alcoholism and Substance Abuse Information Center Hotline

1-800-784-6776

National Suicide Prevention Lifeline

1-800-273-TALK (8255)

INDEX

A Lonely Guy's Guide: How to Deal